Credit Card Debt

An Insider's Secret

Dear reader as a former bankrupt businessman; it is my pleasure to give you a much financial aid as possible, however, I do not have enough finances to pay off the debt of everyone that would read this book. So I would like to offer you the following free gift:

To redeem your free gift simply click upon the link in the Kindle version of this book free with your purchase of this book: it promises to give me your financial independence once again. Get the life you desire at no charge. Let me thank you again for taking this first step towards your freedom and remind you of the giftsimportance

Introduction

Credit cards have been a way of life for some people. Using them in times of emergency, purchasing food, clothing, gas and other needs or wants are some of the things a credit card provide every individual. However, credit cards can also bring financial trouble to one's family; simply because they do not use and manage their credit cards properly.

In our society, the clamor and need to fit in becomes an essential necessity for most people and since credit cards can provide most of the people's "wants", it's easy to fall into the "debt trap".

But all is not lost because there is always hope and help is on your way. Congratulations for purchasing this book. Inside you will find useful tips and guides in making you debt free. I will show you how to manage your money, spend money wisely and so much more. You will have a deeper understanding on how credit card works and more importantly make the credit card work for you and not "YOU" working for it.

Don't worry as you are not alone in battling this problem. There are more people out there who struggle in achieving a debt free status so it's important to be well informed and have the ample knowledge to stop this problem.

Start your journey in setting yourself free. Remember that discipline and commitment is an important key on your road to solving this problem. By the end of this book, it's my aim that you already have the initiative and strength to battle this difficult situation. Learn from your mistakes and make sure that you start your journey for financial freedom.

Read on and be empowered!

Table of Contents

Introduction 3
Chapter 1 - Credit Card: An In-depth Look 6
Chapter 2 - Common Terms of Agreement 9
Chapter 3 - Self-evaluation before a Credit Card Application 12
Chapter 4 - Credit Score and How Credit Card can Affect it 15
Chapter 5 - The Perks of Having a Credit Card 18
Chapter 6 - Credit Card: The Pitfall 21
Chapter 7 - Signs and Symptoms of Heading to a Credit Card Debt 24
Chapter 8 - How to Avoid Credit Card Debt 27
Chapter 9 - How to Reduce your Credit Card Debt 30
Chapter 10 - Credit Card Counseling 33
Conclusion 36

© **Copyright 2014 by AKBpublishing- All rights reserved.**

This document is geared towards providing exact and reliable information in regards to the topic and issue covered. The publication is sold with the idea that the publisher is not required to render accounting, officially permitted, or otherwise, qualified services. If advice is necessary, legal or professional, a practiced individual in the profession should be ordered.

- From a Declaration of Principles which was accepted and approved equally by a Committee of the American Bar Association and a Committee of Publishers and Associations.

In no way is it legal to reproduce, duplicate, or transmit any part of this document in either electronic means or in printed format. Recording of this publication is strictly prohibited and any storage of this document is not allowed unless with written permission from the publisher. All rights reserved.

The information provided herein is stated to be truthful and consistent, in that any liability, in terms of inattention or otherwise, by any usage or abuse of any policies, processes, or directions contained within is the solitary and utter responsibility of the recipient reader. Under no circumstances will any legal responsibility or blame be held against the publisher for any reparation, damages, or monetary loss due to the information herein, either directly or indirectly.

Respective authors own all copyrights not held by the publisher.

The information herein is offered for informational purposes solely, and is universal as so. The presentation of the information is without contract or any type of guarantee assurance.

The trademarks that are used are without any consent, and the publication of the trademark is without permission or backing by the trademark owner. All trademarks and brands within this book are for clarifying purposes only and are the owned by the owners themselves, not affiliated with this document.

Chapter 1 - Credit Card: An In-depth Look

Many people rely mostly in using their credit cards for paying bills, shopping on line and buying other things without the use of cash or check resulting to credit card debt. Credit card debt is a case of unsecured consumer debt which is accessed via credit cards.

History of Credit Card

Before we go to the short history of credit card, do you know what a credit card is and how does it work? Probably some of us do know but others don't since not all people in the world own a card or two.

A credit card is a type of payment card being issued to users as system payment. Cardholders are allowed to pay for the services and goods in exchange of their promise to pay for it. Consumers are allowed a balance of debt which is continuous however it is subjective on the interest that is being charged.

Credit card use started way back 1920's in the United States. It was issued to consumers by individual firms including hotel and large oil companies. It was believed that John Biggins was the one who created the original credit card which was issued by Flatbush National Bank where he worked. He called it "Charge-It" program.

Types of Credit Card

Standard Credit Card is commonly the basic credit card that can be offered by credit card issuer to their customers. Card holder should be at least 18 years of age with good credit and average salary and meets or exceeds the issuer's criteria for minimum credit. There are no deposits required and the credit card issuer establishes the credit limit.

Rewards Card is also a credit card in the sense that it gives you the opportunity of earning different kinds of rewards that are based depending on the usage of a certain rewards card. Rewards may be in the form points, discounts, rebates or even cash. Points earned can be used to purchase goods or services from accredited establishments. Holders should be aware of the limits and restrictions to prevent financial troubles.

Examples of Rewards Card:

Airline/Frequent Flier Miles are cards that earn you airline miles. Accumulated miles can be used for future flight travels. Don't forget that miles have expiration date too.

Cash Back Cards are cards that give back the money you have spent. The range of credit is from 1-5%. Once a minimum amount of credit or cash is collected, you can receive the cash back in the form of a check to pay for your purchase.

Other cards give flat amount of money depending on your total purchase regardless how much is spent, while others have tiers that have different reward levels that depends on your spending.

Point Cards are cards earning you points that you can use to redeem merchandise, gift and entertainment cards. Accumulated points can be used for gassing up, staying at the hotel or for home improvements.

Premium Credit Cards are referred to "upscale" in general. These cards come in "gold" or "platinum" and are offered to customers who have awesome credit standing meaning they have retained that standing for years and is eligible for higher credit limits amounting to at least $10,000.00. Credit card holders of this type have high salaries that spend too much and travel a lot. The annual fees and interest are high. Perks included are exclusive access to airline lounges, auto assistance and around the world travel.

Secured Credit Cards are also known as prepaid debit cards or pay-as-you-go cards. It is a good choice if you find it hard to get a credit card or perhaps you need to repair a bad credit history. This type card has annual fee with annual interest rates that are higher. Oftentimes, they are used for reestablishing your credit. A card holder can only purchase little to have no difficulty in repaying. For a certain period of time of having good payment records it is now possible to acquire a credit card.

Specialty Credit Cards are for the consumers with very special needs for the credit card use. This includes students and business professionals by means of partnerships, service providers, brand retailers or affiliation.

Differences between Visa, MasterCard, Discover and American Express

For us to understand better the differences between these four major credit cards, we will group them in two.

Visa and MasterCard

Both do not issue cards, instead they serve as intermediary organizations that create networks between merchants that provide services and goods and financial companies that include credit unions and major banks issuing cards that bear the logo of Visa or MasterCard name. Issuer (banks) and merchants,payfees for participating in the MasterCard or Visa network. These credit card companies set and keep rules that govern the usage of their branded cards.

American Express and Discover

American Express or Amex (slang) and Discover are similar to one-stop shops. Unlike Visa or MasterCard, they are the ones who issue thy own cards, authorizing purchases and settling both consumers and merchants. The reason for this is because, they are the banks themselves.

Credit Card vs. Debit Card

Both cards looks the same however, there are some differences that you need to keep in mind on how these two cards work.

Money will be deducted directly from your current account (funds that are available) when purchasing using a debit card. Unlike with a credit card purchase, you owe a sum of money that requires to be paid back on a certain date.

Debit cards directly draw money from your checking account upon purchasing. A hold will be placed depending on the amount purchased. The transaction will be sent by the merchants to their bank and is transferred to their account. Always make sure that you keep a running balance to prevent overdraft.

Credit cards on the other hand, enable a cardholder to buy things instantly but to a pre-arranged limit only and pay for it in a later date. Purchase cost will be added to the credit card account providing you every month a statement to monitor your credit card transactions and purchases.

Average credit card of a single person

The average credit card per person is based on his credit score. Of course, if the card holder has a credit score which is excellent, the higher chance of getting more credit cards because of their reputation as a good payer. Unlike with bad credit history, it will take time for him to get approved of a higher amount. He needs to make up with his performance and as soon as he is able to establish a good credit standing that is the time that he will be approved of getting a credit again.

Chapter 2 - Common Terms of Agreement

Ever wonder what does Annual Percentage Rate mean? How about cash advance? Finance Charge? Other fees involved? APR? All jargons and sometimes too much to take in, right? In owning a credit card every consumer should remember that they need to understand what they are getting into. Remember that ignorance is not an excuse especially when it comes to your right as a consumer and the law.

Once you sign your application in acquiring your new credit card, it means that you are agreeing with the terms and conditions of the bank's contract. It is legal, binding and it means that you understand the stipulations that the contract says and will be implemented once signed. Banks often refer them as the cardholder agreement. This document includes important information and all the things you need to know about your credit card. That's the reason why you need to keep them for future reference especially if you have disputes or claims.

So in order to fully understand what you are getting at, let's take a look and review the most common terms that you will find in your agreement:

Annual Percentage Rate (APR) for your Purchases
This is the interest any credit card owner shall be charged on every balance that they don't pay in full on or before the deadline of payment. Some card companies impose different APRs based on different transactions. A good example maybe the rate for your balance transfer which might be lower as against the rate for cash advances.

Balance Transfer
This is the process to transfer one credit to another by using balance transfer. There are some cases that you could be charged a certain fee to complete this process. Fees are normally a percentage of your outstanding balance. Balance transfers don't close your account automatically. You can still choose to continue your account. However, again be careful because in the end you might have more debts instead of just finishing one.

Grace Period
This is the number of days given to the credit card holder in order to pay the full amount on the said due date before accumulating finance charges. This normally ranges from 20-30 days which is according to FDIC or the Federal Deposit Insurance Corporation. However, it's quite difficult to find a credit card that gives a grace period for balance transfers or cash advances. Most credit card companies do not give any grace period at all.

Cash Advance

Cash advances are instant loan given by any credit card companies. This is a convenient way of getting instant cash especially during emergencies. It is done by simply accessing any ATM or can be provided through what is called "convenience checks" which will be provided by the credit card issuer. This however has a higher interest rate than your regular purchases and interest rates start immediately on the day you took the cash advance.

Claims and Disputes

This is your right as a consumer to ask, double check the charges or if there are discrepancies on your billing statement. Make sure that you have the necessary supporting documents in case a dispute is at hand. Contact them via the address written on your agreement or through their customer service hotline. Some of the common disputes include over charges, identity theft, fraud, incorrect charges or person who uses the card without the owner's knowledge.

Fees

Here are some of the fees that you will encounter in your credit card statements.

- **Annual Fee:** Yearly fee being charged to any card holder. Some cards provide other benefits such as points, miles, freebees, rewards or in some cases minimal insurance coverage.

- **Late Fee:** Fees imposed when payment is not received on time. According to the CARD Act rule that took effect on the early 2010, payments that are made by 5pm on the said deadline shall be considered not late and on time.

Note: The CARD Act is also called the Credit Cardholders Bill of Rights which was signed by President Obama last May 2009. Most significant provisions stipulated on this Act took effect on February 2010.

- **Over-the-Limit Fee:** A fee that is charged when you've already exceeded your credit limit. There are some credit card companies that have already eliminated this fee.

Finance Charge

These are charges included when a consumer did not pay their bills on or before the deadline. Typically, consumers are given a grace period (which was discussed on previous bullet) or a time in order for them to settle their accounts. However, once it's already past due, these charges are immediately applied on their account.

Computation of the Balance of Purchases

This is the process on how all transactions are being computed together with the card owner's monthly remaining balance. For example: if the processuses the "average daily balance," it means that everyday's transactions will be added to the running balance, which will be divided by the total amount of days in the card owner's billing cycle.

Minimum Payment

This is the lowest amount of payment a card owner has to pay every month to avoid late fees and be in default. As much as possible pay more to pay the debt faster and interest rates will also be lesser.

Billing Cycle

This is the period between your billings. Certain billings may start on the every 1st of the month and will end by the 30th of the month. Cycles vary in lengths – either from 20-45days, depending on the credit card companies. In the billing cycle, fees, purchases, credits and charges are all posted on your account. By the end of the cycle, a statement will be generated and all the information will be shown on said document.

Transaction Fee

A term to describe fees charged for different types of transactions, like balance transfer, regular purchases, purchases made on other countries and cash advance. The percentage of computation is based the total amount of all transactions.

Understanding these usual terms and conditions before using your credit card is important. Remember that this is a legal document and whatever is stipulated on it should be implemented. However there is that issue of "fine print" that most creditors forget to inform the consumers. It is important to be vigilant and well-informed because this would eventually save you from getting deep into credit card debts.

Chapter 3 – Self-evaluation before a Credit Card Application

People tend to be amazed and overwhelmed with the numerous offers from different companies and bank institutions that offer credit cards. It is best to evaluate yourself first before going on your credit card application to avoid problems that may come your way in the future. The offers are overwhelming but you have to think about it not just for once but as many times as you think you should.

Why do you need it?

Always bear in mind that a credit card may be a source of temptation in spending more than you are able to pay your debt. You should consider different views and the possibilities as it may take you to a situation that will cause you stress in paying your monthly bill before you continue and signing a credit card application.

- **Think about it many times over. Why do you need a credit card?**

    1. *You wanted to use it to shop for new clothes, shoes, etc.* – Do you really need to spend for these material things? How important is it for you to have the latest type of rubber shoes? Probably, you are just attracted with the newest designs from your favorite designer. Your closet maybe full with unused blouses and pants. It is true especially for women like you to buy things that you do not really need. Avoid being an impulsive buyer as you may only waste your money.

    2. *You wanted to do some cash advances* – credit cards offer cash advance but have you considered the mechanics on how you should pay for it? A bigger amount of cash advance means bigger monthly bill. How about the basic needs you need the most? Do you still have an enough amount to buy them when the need arises?

    3. *You wanted to use it for worry-free dine-outs* – dining-out is always good as long as you can pay for your bill. Your credit card may be of great help in treating out your loved ones or some friends. It is not bad to use it provided you know if you can still survive paying the amount you are required in the coming months.

Be careful and wise in selecting a credit card

It is not right to grab all the offers for a credit card application. You might be confused with the perks they are giving you. You may end up a loser in the end especially when you don't know how to control your expenses done in using it. Take into considerations the following points so you will be on the right track in selecting a credit card that fits your needs.

- **Pointers to consider**

    1. *Know about the interest rate* – the interest rate used for different purchases may vary. It is important to know them so you would be able to calculate its effect on your bill. The annual cost of credit which is commonly known as annual percentage rate (APR) should be monitored as it goes with economic conditions. It is better if you can negotiate for a lesser amount of APR.

    2. *Learn about annual fees and other charges* – the annual fees are usually charged on the date closest to the anniversary when you are granted the credit card. A credit card that charges lower annual fee is great. Please be conscious that there are some other fees that maybe charged at your end depending on your credit rating such as the following:

        o Activation fee
        o Participation fee
        o Acceptance fee
        o Cash advance fee
        o Balance transfer fee

    3. *Remember the terms given for grace periods* – it is regularly given for 20 to 30 days which still makes you free from interest charges. It can help you is you can find a credit card that offers longer grace period to keep you away from charges and instead, can save you some amount of money.

    4. *Be knowledgeable in computing the outstanding balance and finance charges* – most of the credit card companies use the ADB or average daily balance method. The computation is done by dividing your daily sum balance by the term thus, leaving the newest purchases at the moment. The payments already made are considered making finance charges lower. You have to check the methods which are done by other companies called as the double ADB method as it is incurs the highest computation of interest and

finance charges. The method uses the ADB total from your two month-billing cycle.

Types of credit card users

To which type of credit card users do you belong? Are you one of the non-revolvers or do you belong to the revolvers? You can be one of the combination users instead!

- *Non-revolvers* – these are the credit card users who always pay their balance in full amount every month. Some of them use their cards strictly for business transactions and travels. In doing this method, you are sure to be free from other charges. You are considered wise if you belong to this type of credit card user but financial standing counts a lot.
- *Revolvers* – they are the people who opt to pay the exact amount for minimum payments or just have a little over it. Their credit card balance is carried out every month making them pay for higher interest charges. In here belong the regular earners with carefully computed monthly budget.
- *Combination Users* – this type is the combination of both. They normally pay the minimum balance and they can always have just a few months to pay their balance in full. People who fall into this type are luckier than the revolvers because they can somehow avoid the charges. It can be done if you know how to forecast and compute you expenses together with the money you will earn to pay your bill.

The approved credit card application means you are bound to be responsible in making your purchases and paying your bills. Think wisely and check the negative things that might cause you problems as well as the positive things it may brought you before you apply for a credit card.

Chapter 4 - Credit Score and How Credit Card can Affect it

Credit score is a dynamic part in a borrower's credit health influencing the available credit and terms lenders could offer. There are a lot of factors that affect the credit card score.

History of Payment

Missing your payments or paying late will greatly damage your credit score which take up to seven years getting a hit, for some certain items it can take up to ten years. If all your bills and balances are paid on time, your payment history remains clean that will results in higher score. However, paying late will result to a lot of consequences:

Late Fee Charges. Creditors charge late fees. Late fees will usually charge from $15 to $35, which depends whether it's the first time you paid late within the past six months. For each month that you missed a payment, will also be the number of late charge fees.

Increased Interest Rate. If within 60 days, you are delinquent, the interest rate will increase. You are not only penalized for late fees but your interest rate for the penalty rate will increase as well. Higher interest rate will make your finance charges more expensive for carrying a balance.

Late payment adds to credit report if more than 30 days late. It will be added to your credit report which can stay for seven years. If the next payment is missed, it will be updated to 60 days up until to 180 days the account will be charged off.

Your credit score will fluctuate. Since 35% of the credit score makes up the payment history, paying late will have a great effect on your score that affects the ability of getting new credit in the future. The better your credit, the better your credit score standing.

Credit History

Your credit history is not easily changed by the length of time that you have credit access. Creditor checks the trends in your payment patterns likewise with the credit applications in your account. Even if a cardholder has good history credit to boost his ratings, his credit score will still decrease if he applies for new credit or habitually miss his payments.

Existing Debts

Your credit score card will definitely go down if you have high balances on several cards in relation to your total credit limit.

Type of Existing Credit

It is considerably healthier to have a car loan, home equity loan, mortgage and one or two credit cards than to have multiple credit cards. Aiming for the correct balance between these types of credit will make an improvement on the credit score.

Definition of a credit card

Credit card is a very suitable substitute for check or cash which is also a necessary component of electronic and internet commerce. It is a plastic token with a usual size of 3 3/8 x 2 1/8 inches. It has a magnetic stripe holding a machine code which is readable. It allows consumers a continuous debt balance which is subject to the interest that is being charged. In general, third party who is engaged with the transactions and pays the seller which is being reimbursed by the buyer in return.

Different credit card score

Credit card score is a document detailing the personal history of a borrower of how he handles borrowed money. It is a 3-digit number reflecting credit card report information. The significance of having a credit score will help lenders or creditors in evaluating an individual how risky is he as a borrower.

With this, a system of how to grade a credit score has been developed. This is called the Vantage Score Range. The letter grades that you will see are like those grades from the school where "A" is excellent and "F" is worse or failed. It ranges from 501 to 990. The higher is the score, the better for a borrower.

901 - 900 = A (Super Prime)

801 – 900 = B (Prime Plus)

701 – 800 = C (Prime)

601 – 700 = D (Non-Prime)

501 – 600 = F (High Risk)

Effect of credit card to your credit card score

Closing a credit card reduces all of your accounts average age hurting your credit score. Likewise with closing your credit card account and getting more debt will give credit score the same effect which is negative.

This will also contributes great effect on your credit utilization ratio which pertains to the probability of credit available you are using already. The credit limit and credit which is still available will be reported as totally $0, which seems you have maxed out.

How to maintain a good credit score

Knowledge of what makes a good credit score. It is important that you know about things that makes a good credit score. There are fivenecessary pieces informationused to calculate credit score. These are debt level,current credit, mix of credit and loan, history of payment and age of the credit.

Prompt payment of the bills. We are talking about here all of your bills not only the bills for loans or credit card. Even a small amount of bill left unpaid will add to your credit report. Pay all of your bills on time for good credit score maintenance and you will be thankful for the benefits that you can get such as improved credit score, make your account stayed out of collections, take advantage of lower interest rates, and lower insurance rates while keeping your credit score in good standing.

Keeping credit card balances low. Credit score will be worse if you have a credit balance that is higher. It should only be around 30% of the credit limit for a maintained good credit score. If you close your statement and have a high balance, creditors generally report it affecting your credit score greatly even if the balance is paid in full.

Debt management. Not only credit card balances affect credit card score but also lines of credit and loan balances. Too much debt will likely cost credit card score making it hard to pay monthly bills. Lowering your debt, make it easier for a maintained good credit score standing.

Do not close your old credit cards.

Limit for new credit card applications. Every new application either for a credit card or loan will surely lessen your credit score aside from lowering your credit age average which is 15% of your average score. For a maintained good credit score, you should be frugal in opening new accounts.

Eyeing your credit report. Even though you are meticulous about everything with your credit does not mean that everyone do the same. Mistakes sometimes happen that could end up in a drop in your credit score. Regular checking of your credit card report enables you to discover these errors and correct it.

Chapter 5 - The Perks of Having a Credit Card

Since you were approved of a Credit Card and you actually have the physical card with you. What will you do next? Are you excited to make your first purchase?

Here's a guide that will help you determine what to do with your card and how you can maximize its usage. Read it carefully and be amazed on the wonders of your card.

Why people cannot live without them?

Credit cards are one of the most used cards today. You can practically buy anything using it. You just need to activate it, find the item you like and make a purchase. Many people can't live without it because it can be used in different ways like when make big purchases- you don't need to pay the full amount. You can opt to pay the minimum payment instead. There are a lot of advantages in using a Credit Card. Here are some of them:

Convenience. Most people utilize it nowadays because it's very convenient for them. You don't need to bring too much cash with you when you need to buy something.

Fast and Reliable. If you are good credit card payer all transactions will be fast and consistent. Everything will be hassle free.

Record purchases. One of the things we like about Credit Cards is its ability to record your transactions. You will see the cards' advantages especially when you forgot the date and place of you purchased item.

Online transactions. People are often hooked on buying hard to find items online. It's easier to buy things using this. There are many online shops that accept cards as a payment.

Avoid Fraud. We know there are a lot of fraudsters around. When you make transactions using your card, you can dispute unauthorized purchases so you won't be deducted for it.

Good side of getting a credit card

Using credit cards also has a lot of perks. It is not only used to pay for something. You will be surprised that you will receive a lot of benefits when you acquire one.

Earn Rewards. The best thing about credit cards is that you earn points for its usage. These points can be used for making transactions in the future like in travelling. Points accumulated from your frequent travels can be added to your payment. So it means the more you travel, the more opportunities to travel for free. You can also get points when you make payment, especially for big purchases like when you buy appliances. If you have accumulated many points it can even be used to pay for your annual membership fee.

PrivilegePass. In some events, credit card users get a free or a VIP pass especially if you are a Gold, Silver or Platinum card holders. You are entitled to acquire the best seats, access VIP lounges and get more perks than those without credit cards.

Freebies. What card holders like about Credit card is being able to get free items on purchases. For example some restaurants provide a free meal or dessert when you pay using a specific credit card.

Special Discounts. In some business establishments' credit card holders who show or pay using a particular credit card get special discounts. Sometimes the special discounts come on top or their regular discount. So imagine the money that you save when you go shopping or when you dine-out.

Installment feature. This is the best thing about credit cards. Imagine being able to pay tuition fees, multiple purchases and pay it within 6-12 months. You can pay for a lot of items in installment basis. How can you refuse this offer especially if it's zero interest? Some even has a buy now, pay later plan. You can purchase the item now and pay 2-3 months after.

Cash Advance. Account holders are also attracted with the Cash Advance feature where you can withdraw the money you need immediately. All you need to know is the PIN id and you'll get instant cash fast and worry free.

Cash Returns. Most card companies offer this feature that allows you to gain at least 1 % of the amount you purchased. It's like a money back feature so you pay less.

Buyer Protection. Some companies have a buyer protection plan paid with a very minimal fee. This protects you from bogus seller, damaged and defective items. Since it can be used for online buying this is the common problem that you are protected with.

Building Credit History. When you apply for loan with banks, information that they need to assess is your credit card history. The usage of your credit will help build your credit score especially when you pay your dues on time.

Worry Free Travel. Bringing a lot of cash when you travel is not always a good idea. It is best to use credit cards. In that way you won't need to always go to a money changer to have your money changed to the currency of the country you are in. The company will automatically do it for you. So you will have fewer worries.

Insurance. This is the best feature for some credit cards because it helps you in case of accidents and even protects your credit cards when it gets stolen. Some companies offer medical insurance and assistance in case you get hospitalized for certain diseases. Most of the time you only need to pay a very minimal fee or it comes free if you have reached a certain reward point. In case your credit card gets stolen too, do not be afraid. If you signed up for their insurance policy, you don't have to pay for unauthorized transactions.

So you see there are great deals that you can do with your credit cards. It such an advantage to have one. Use it to finance your children's education, since there are a lot of schools that offer credit card payment. Others use it to pay for their rent, medical insurance, mortgage and a lot more. If you are a good credit card payer your credit card limit will increase and you will enjoy more privileges that you can never imagine.

Chapter 6 - Credit Card: The Pitfall

In the previous chapter you've seen the different perks of having a credit card and what benefits it could give someone. But, are you responsible enough to handle those perks? In today's economy, people accumulate debt all the time and it is slowly becoming a norm among younger generations. Credit cards are not about having fun and spending money that you don't have, you should know how and when to use it properly. So let's dive in a little a bit further into the pitfall so that you can see what happens when you don't manage your finances properly.

How you fall in debt?

There are a number of reasons why people accumulate debt; it could be because of medical reasons, unemployment or sudden death of a relative. But, most of the time it's associated with bad spending habits. A credit card is like a friend who lends you a hand in buying something that you can pay at a later time and promises you that the terms of payment are going to be easy and light on the pocket. However, the sad reality of this is you only end up owing more. The lack of knowledge in managing your debts can make your credit balances static, therefore resulting in a huge amount of debt.

Here's a sample situation, imagine purchasing a $500 item that is paid at $15 monthly. The monthly payment is very manageable, but what you don't know is the interest rate behind your purchase. Most of the credit card nowadays has bigger interest rate. But, it doesn't just end there, you still have to pay for your financed homeand car, for college and weddings and to top that off there are those emergency medical conditions or unemployment. As you can see, debt can accumulate very fast. The reason why most people get into huge debt will involve personal and impersonal finances.

Another reason why people get into debt is when a person spends more than what they can afford. This is especially true for the younger generations. Living within your monthly paychecks is ideal, but it is rarely achieved. Another is, not reviewing the monthly statement and completely disregarding it, if you are unable to pay for the month, do not ignore it try to manage and plan ahead. If you can, try to pay more than the minimum, because the longer you pay a balance, the bigger the money you will owe.

Even the most brilliant and thrifty person can easily go into debt in just a blink of an eye. So the best thing to do in these situations is to have an emergency savings account that is worth 6 months or more of your salary, in this way you are still capable of paying your credit card bills even if you become unemployed or if you encounter any unforeseen medical emergencies.

Downside of Having a Credit Card:

For every advantage there is an equivalent disadvantage. Credit cards are very convenient if you know how to manage your monthly bills, but there are also various downsides of having a credit card and it can really put you in a great deal of stress , here are some good examples:

- Overspending – Because of the convenience that a credit card offers to its owners, it may feel overwhelming to purchase using a credit card because you don't hand over cash. It makes you feel like you are not spending any money. But, at the end of every month you receive a bill with the total amount of everything you've purchased within the given month which may be more that what you could afford and lead you to incur debt, fees, and a bad credit

- Credit card fraud – There is a possibility that your account information can be stolen. This will allow a person to make purchases under your card and under your name. And if you do not monitor your account regularly you may not notice these unfamiliar charges.

- Interest charges – If you fail to pay your charges your card will incur interest which may take you a little more extra time to clear your charges and end up costing you more.

- Bad Credit – If you have abused or over used your cards' limit, your credit score will go into downward spiral and your credit reputation will be destroyed

- Too much card – People with an existing card will have a considerably easier time in applying a new card. But, this can also lead a person to get numerous cards which is bad in the eyes of lenders.

- Possible bankruptcy – Studies show that a credit card debt is one of the factors contributing to bankruptcies of some individuals.

Here are some tips for handling your credit card:

- Keep your receipts – Be very vigilant about your billing statement and try to compare your receipt with your charges to check for any unfamiliar charges on your card.

- Budget – Avoid bringing you card everywhere with you so that you can avoid unnecessary or impulsive purchases. Budget your money wisely; your card should always be your last resort.

- Pay on time - Make an effort to make payments before the deadline to avoid any late charges and high interest rates.

- Online shopping – Be sure to only do online shopping with reputable websites. Make sure that the website starts with 'https' because these indicates that you are in a secured website. This is also to protect you from credit card fraud.

- Avoid limited time offerings – Some credit card companies offer teaser rates, or low introductory price for a particular product, avoid getting these or applying for these because once the promo ends you'll end up with a big charge on your bill that you may not be able to keep up.

- Report stolen credit cards immediately

Having a credit card is an advantage and they offer a great deal of convenience for the owner. However, be very careful because this can land you in a position you don't want to be in. Being a disciplined card holder is the key to avoid being in debt.

Chapter 7 - Signs and Symptoms of Heading to a Credit Card Debt

Credit cards have been a way of life for some individuals. It's convenient, fast and can be used anywhere, anytime. It's an easy way of making a payment. However, many fell into the pitfalls of purchasing things that are not necessarily needed in their lives. This promotes "impulse buying" – like seeing a good pair of shoes, expensive clothes, gadgets that you already have and eventually, you'll be surprised that your bills have already piled up! *Tsk...tsk....tsk.......*in the end, you are still held responsible in making those payments.

Using your credit cards unwisely and relentlessly can lead to a lot of credit card debts that would eventually be impossible to overcome. An important step that you can do in order to avoid being deeply indebted and be a victim of this problem is to know when and how to stop. You should be able to recognize the signs that you are beginning to fall into a serious credit card debt. The question is what are the signs and symptoms?

- **Using your credit card to meet your basic needs**
  The wages and the earnings you accumulate every month should be enough in buying your needs like food, gas and clothes. If you are always using your credit card to cover up on these purchases then this means that you are in a financial crisis. Do not live beyond your means and find ways to add more income in your family earnings.

- **Transferring balances to avoid payments**
  Balance transfers for your credit cards are often a good way in ridding of your credit card debts and consolidating them to get a much lower interest. However, if you do that more often, chances are you end up adding another credit card and may eventually use it again instead of just maintaining one. This also means that you don't have enough funds to fully pay out your balance on the existing one. Figure out a way to make sure that you have enough to pay your credit card debt every month.

- **Avoiding your credit card statements**
  If you think that you can forget about your debts or payments, then guess again! Intentionally forgetting or ignoring your credit card statements will not help you in paying your debts. This would only worsen and hurt you more if you keep on skipping your payments. Remember that interest grows and this would only make your debts higher.

- **Skipping a credit card bill to pay for another loan**
  If this has been your situation for quite some time then this signals trouble. Being strapped or short for cash means that you need to do

something about it. If you can't keep up with paying your monthly bills then it means that your income does not match your spending habits. Do not skip your payments as this would definitely hurt your credit score leaving you with less and less options in paying your debts.

- **Making minimum payments only to your credit card due**
  This is an alarming sign that your credit card balance will eventually balloon and accumulate more interest and fees. Paying only the minimum amount for your card will not reduce the balance significantly. In order to avoid such demise, its better that you can pay more than the minimum payment so that you can also pay your credit card debts faster.

- **You are having a difficult time in saving because most of your money goes to your credit card payments**
  All of your earnings are not enough to settle your monthly bills therefore you are starting to use your savings to make sure that you can make the payment. This situation is very common especially for people who have more than one credit card. So make sure to control and spend wisely. As much as possible, retain only one credit card so that you will not have a difficult time in making your payments monthly.

- **Using your credit card to buy expensive items**
  The temptation of buying things that you can't afford is laid out in front of you. People have a habit of buying expensive things that they don't really need. In order to maintain a certain "status quo", people are trying hard to meet and keep up with what is dictated by the society and once you fall prey into this kind of thinking, you will definitely have a hard time becoming debt free.

- **Maxing out your credit card limit**
  A sure sign that you are having financial difficulties is when you keep on using your credit card and using it all out. This means that your income is not enough to buy things that you need therefore opting to use your credit card often. Eventually, your balance continue to remain the same and you end up paying more interest and charges lessening the chance of paying for your credit card debt.

- **Using your credit card because you expect that you will have a large income in the future**
  Finding yourself in using your card for big purchases because you expect that you will have the money for it is not a good idea. It's not right to charge or buy something before you actually have the money on hand or you have already earned it. Spend your money wisely in order to avoid more debts.

- **Your request for a credit limit increase is constantly declined**

If you kept on requesting for an increase on credit limit and eventually being declined, there is a strong indication that you have been spending much more than what you can afford. Credit card providers can determine your credit worthiness by just looking at your spending habits. If your request for an increase is constantly being declined, then it means these companies know that you won't be able to handle more. In the end, they might be doing you a favor.

- **Being stressed and constantly worried about your debts**
  Managing your financial status can be stressful however having a huge debt and finding ways to pay it off is more stressful. So if you think that you are constantly worrying and losing so much sleep because of your debts, and then take it as a warning sign to start making the necessary adjustments in your financial situation. Remember that in order for you to earn money, you need to have good health and being stressed does not have the making of a healthy life.

If you feel that you are already seeing these warning signs, it's time for you to make a change. Re-think and evaluate your spending habits and manage your financial situation. Remember that the longer you linger and wait, the harder it is to solve your financial woes.

Chapter 8 - How to Avoid Credit Card Debt?

Now that you have an overview on what is a credit card, how it works and if you think that it's the best for you – it's about time to know how to avoid being in too deep with your credit card debt. Though there are some advantages of having a credit card, be aware that there are also disadvantages. Resisting the urge to use your credit card is a big responsibility and requires a lot of self control. Remember the movie "Confessions of a Shopaholic"? The main character had a hard time resisting the urge to use her credit card to the point that she is already addicted and way too deep in debt. Now, my friend, if you are starting to experience these symptoms yourself, then it's time for you to evaluate your spending habits and know how well you manage your money.

Money& Loan Management

Hard as we try, for some reason most of us are not exactly successful in managing our financial situation. We fall prey to living beyond our means and being an impulsive buyer. To make sure that we use our credit cards appropriately, here are some of the tips that I find useful to ensure that I managed my money and loan well:

- **Don't use your credit card if you think you can't afford to pay them on time:** A lot of consumers overlook the need to control their spending habits. In the end, they swipe and swipe their card away not thinking of the consequence on how to pay it back come billing schedule.
- **Avoid availing the cash advances:** As much as possible, steer clear of using your credit card to get cash. Most of the time financial companies give a higher interest if you get cold cash using your credit card. Aside from that, interest is already starting once you get the cash. So even if you have already paid the amount in full, you still have to pay for the interest that goes with availing the cash.
- **Create your budget:** One of the best ways to keep track of your spending habit is to write down all your expenses, monthly bills and other payables every month. This way you'll be able to know if you have already spent too much and will also know how much resources are still available so that you can make the necessary adjustments.
- **Use your credit card for emergency purposes only:** While it's really hard to be debt-free, there are instances that we can't avoid having an emergency in our family. Since, you don't have enough cash at the moment; your credit card is the best option. However, once you use it make sure that you will have a plan on how to go about making the payment to avoid piling up the debt on your credit card.
- **Make sure to make your payment on time:** One of the pitfalls of getting deep into credit card debt is either skipping your monthly payment or being late in making that payment. In order to avoid these problems,

make sure that you already allot the budget to pay for your credit card bills on time. Remember that once you skip or be late in payments, charges also pile up like interest, late fees and others. This would definitely add up if you are not mindful with the schedule of your payments.

- **Try to pay your balance in full:** This is a good practice because once you pay-off your credit card balance in full; you will avoid being charged interest rates and other fees.
- **Avoid having too many credit cards:** It's really simple, the more credit cards you have, the more bills you will pay every month. So make sure that you can only "bite in what you can chew" to keep away from being in debt trouble. After all, you don't need too many cards. As long as you really know how to manage your payment, everything will be okay.
- **Make a record of your purchases:** This is the only way you will be able to keep track of your expenses. Aside from that, this is a fool proof way of back-tracking all the things you've spent – because sometimes there's a tendency to forget what we've purchased in the last couple of weeks or months.
- **Reading the fine print:** Most people take for granted the terms of agreement they are entering into. They do not read or ask questions if they don't understand the things stated on it. So to further avoid being in a compromising situation, make sure that you read and understood what is stated in the agreement like interest rates, fees, charges. Be vigilant and well informed on that matter.
- **Finally, you may want to leave your credit card at home:** An effective way to resist temptation is to keep it out of reach. If you think that you have enough cash to spend, leave your credit card to avoid overspending and using your credit card.

Good vs. Bad Debts

Avoiding debts is a good way to prepare for a stress-free and stable financial future. However, there are times that we can't avoid entering into a debt. Getting a car plan, housing loans or even the children's college education is something that would make us enter into loans. However, some people can't help but overlook and make things out of hand in terms of managing their debts.

While it's kinda hard to avoid debt, the challenging part is how to judge or decide what debt makes sense in your spending schedule or not. Aside from that, which of these debts are categorically a good or a bad debt in your life?

Good debts are things that you really need but don't have enough cash or can't afford to pay for it at the moment. These debts include car loans, college education or housing loans. These types of loans require a fixed monthly schedule of payment and it should be well-managed and included in your monthly budget.

Now bad debts on the other hand, are those that you really don't need. They can be planned ahead or at least you can try to save up for them so that you will avoid getting into debt. Some examples maybe going to a vacation to Paris or Hawaii, buying expensive clothes that you don't need or wear too often – and the worst debt of all is using your credit card too much.

In the end, only you can control and manage your money. While it's easier said than done, giving excuses will also not help us in moving along with our lives. You don't have to change right away. The most important thing is you try it out and learn from your mistakes.

Chapter 9 - How to Reduce your Credit Card Debt

We all know how much people succumbed to having everything they want. People are naturally hoarders and materialistic. Even they don't really need it as long as they have a current addiction and want to possess them, the buying habit will continue and this is one of the reasons why credit card invented.

Financial institution's experts realized the demand of consumers to get hold of the things they want and need, but the predicament of acquiring all with cash is not favorable. What a consumer need is a flexible payment terms to carry the load of her or his bill payment. Before there where loan investment programs which is still very much available today, but still there's more suitable payment terms for everyone.

So, when an idea of credit cards came to view, this is like an answered prayer.

The Procedure

Of course, there are certain rules to follow and the process must take accordingly. Important documents like employment certificates, proof of billing, tax certificate and Identification cards like driver's license or legit company id are one of the constant requirements to submit before a person can avail a credit card.

One of the significant reasons is to diligently know the person who will become a credit card holder. This is actually a standard office procedure when you're availing anybenefit program from a financial establishment. As you know, this is also one way to protect the institution from fraud transactions. Since there is hundreds of credit card application everyday they need to verify the legitimacy of all the credit card applicants.

The Realization of Credit Card

Ever since credit card came to view, nothing is impossible to avail. The buying freedom of consumers is finally realized. This is indeed a glorious moment to celebrate. Commercial markets are tying up with the credit card institution to come up with such strategy to make people patronize their products on sale. Schemes like zero interest, low interest rates or lowest payment terms offered to all major credit card holders.

This is again another reason to celebrate. For consumers who are addicted to mobile phones or any other user-friendly devices are easily hooked with these kinds of credit card marketing schemes. The buying power of credit cards do not only entertain product buying thus it also applies to restaurants, supermarkets and yes even for your utility bills. True enough credit cards became the best solution to pay off your financial obligations.

However, because it's very helpful and handy, people become abusive from the benefits of credit card. The downside of this unacceptable manner is the point of the card holder being drowned with debts. If you don't know yet the real drama of credit cards, it is actually putting your financial management at risk.

You're blinded to the reality of investing your money to pay the debt obligation all your life. Just because you're enjoying "get the item now and pay later" you don't seem to understand the real purpose of credit card. There's nothing really wrong about availing a credit card, everyone has the right to do so.

That's why before you're trapped in the pitfall of debts; you must become truly aware of the consequence of your action when using your credit card.

Make a plan

Like what the above statement is saying, you need to calm yourself to be able to plan the right approach to settle your credit card problem. It's not really advisable to go bankrupt, thus it's better to have options and there's a lot to choose from when doing so.

Do not make any senseless moves like locking inside your room or avoiding calls and visitors because you're afraid it must be the creditors or the repo man. Planning your way out from your credit card debt can become very stressful, but you can always come up with a better plan how to deal with it. Here are two things you can do;

Gather all information – as part of your planning you need to gather all your credit card debt information like transaction slip, statement of account and the contact information of your credit card company. These three things are important when you're planning to settle your credit card debts. Make sure it is well-kept where you can find it easily, just in case you already need it.

Make a list – write down the possible resources you can ask for financial help. You can include your immediate family, your close friends or even your employer. It's not actually you'll be asking for financial aid per se, but you just need a good advice from people whom you know will truly understand your present ordeal. The hardest part to ask for help is when you have money problems. Most of them will make you instead of helping you. So, make sure that those people, you will ask for help is good enough to extend whatever help they can offer without taunting you.

Payment or settlement strategies (how to payoff)

Sit down with your credit card company agent – One of the best waysis taking the honest action to inform your creditors about your current financial status why you cannot pay your credit card bills lately. Tell them that you're a long time subscriber of their credit card company. For some company they're glad to hear that, but for others who don't really care is going to become a problem, but of course credit card companies are always ready for this kind of situation that's why they already have generic arrangements to finish off their subscriber's debt to them.

Does some personal inventory – why not try to do some personal inventory. Meaning check out the possible things you can dispose to raise some money to pay off your debt. This may count as the desperate move, but forpractical reasons, you know you have some valuables stored in your home that you don't really need. And for some reasons it has significant market value. Post it on your social network sites and wait for a day or two a potential buyer will message you.

Chapter 10 - Credit Card Counseling

Credit Card counseling is a common process helping every single debtor that have to settle their debts by educating them how to budget and wisely use the variety of tools with the goal of reducing and eliminating debt for good. This is also known as Debt Counseling in United Kingdom frequently done Credit counseling agencies enabled by contract acting on debtor's behalf in negotiating with creditors in resolving debt because debtor is having difficulty in paying that is beyond his ability.

Agencies which can help

There are a lot of agencies that can help you with your financial situation. Most are "non-profit" but it does not mean that the service or services they offer are affordable, free or conform to the law. As a matter of fact, some will charge high hidden fees or make their clients to pay what they called as 'voluntary' contributions causing additional debt.

Association of Independent Consumer Credit Counseling Agencies and National Foundation for Credit Counseling is the two specialized agencies representing Credit counselors in the United States. Federal Trade Commission or FTC is the one who regulates Credit counseling and serves as the protector of the consumer against companies who deceive them about the benefits of their different services, nature and cost.

Financial Conduct Authority. This agency is based in the United Kingdom and is accountable in regulating consumer credit. They had created a Debt Management Plan and can charge fine for misconduct.

Swedish Confederation of Professional Employees implements guidelines used for credit counseling, encouraging creditors to use them instead of court system. Based in Ireland is the *Irish Congress of Trade Unions or ICTU* that provides debtors directly with the information on debt resolution. *LAKRA* which is based in Latvia is a debt advisory company that works with the employers assisting employees that are in debt. All these agencies comprise the European Union Credit counseling agencies which are widely varied of the regulating and non-regulating Credit services which include DMPs.

Financial Consumer Agency of Canada or FCAC is located of course in Canada. This advised Canadians to research first about Credit counseling services before deciding to accept an agreement. Consumers should check and compare services of various counseling bodies. They have to see the difference in the construction of the fees of the profit and non-profit credit counseling likewise with the services offered that comes along with the said fees.

National Credit Regulator or NCR takes responsibility in the regulation of credit industry in South Africa. This Act was established under the National Credit Act

No. 34 of 2005 as a regulator. Its task is to register credit providers, debt counselors and credit bureau and enforce compliance of the Act.

Other Tips

These are some of the things you need to be meticulous about to know if you really are getting the help that you need from your chosen credit counseling agency:

Know what services they offer. Choose an organization which offers a wide range of service like savings and debt management as well as budget counseling. Any organization telling you that Debt Management Plan is your only choice, should be dodged before suggestive amount of time is spent studying your financial status.

Be careful of the agencies claiming that they can negotiate with your creditors making you pay only a part of your debt. This is called "debt negotiation" or "debt settlement". Some services may be misrepresented by these companies stating that what they offer is a part of government program which is not true.

Comfort level with your credit counselor. Make sure that you do not have any uneasy feelings towards your credit counselor and you are assured of his judgment and conviction. Trust is very important and without it nothing can be solved. If in any case you are not comfortable enough with the counselor assigned to help you, another counselor can be requested to help you with your status.

Contracts that is easy to understand. You should have a clear understanding before agreeing to any contract. It should inform you how much will be the fees, what will be your responsibilities, what are your expectations from the agency and when will your payments get processed. You should know what to expect if there is a change in financial circumstances and you cannot make payments anymore. Do not be afraid to ask questions if there are things you do not fully understand especially the terms and conditions. Do not sign anything or agreed just like that without seeking the company's reputation with the help of your trusted sources. Most of all, do not forget to get a copy of the contract for self-keeping.

While still on a Debt Management Plan. Debt Management Plan is depositing your money monthly with the chosen credit counseling organization. These deposits are then used in paying your unsecured debts in accordance to the agreed schedule of payment between you and your creditors. These unsecured debts include student loans, medical bills, car loans and credit cards bills.

While being on the management plan, your debt maybe reduced by creditor. They could give you interest rate which is lower, which saves you money. It's just that you may be charged for the agency's services. If you see that you are paying more for the service fees than saving, it would be better to ask for help from other agencies.

Your progress and payments should be monitored. Reports in the form of written status maybe requested from the agency however they may stop sending you these reports if you are still under the debt management program. If statements are still received, carefully review it to check that the agency really paying the creditor promptly, avoiding late fees or any unsatisfactory records to your credit report.

In monitoring your progress, a copy of this credit report can be requested giving you the opportunity to check if all of the information are correct and if there are any mistakes, it can be corrected as soon as possible.

Conclusion

Great job in finishing this book! I hope that you have learned so much from this journey to become a "smart" credit card user. Now that you have finished the entire book, it's time for you to put it in use. Follow the simple guidelines that were mentioned in the book. Become more disciplined and as always learn from your mistake. If you think that you won't be able to pick up yourself from these credit card debts, then you are mistaken. Don't lose hope and keep a positive attitude.

Keep in mind that you can always go back and read this book again to get guidance and empowerment. Make it a habit to remind yourself that gaining financial freedom is an utmost importance in your life. Take note that if you have your family, financial stability is important as they will be relying on you for the future to come.

Do not procrastinate and do your best to get rid of those temptations that would eventually lead you to your financial downfall. Be content with what you have and do not live beyond your means.

Again, thanks for purchasing this book. Be sure to share your wonderful experience and if you enjoyed this book, please take the time to share your thoughts and post a review on Amazon. It'd be greatly appreciated!

Good luck! Use your credit card wisely!

www.ingramcontent.com/pod-product-compliance
Lightning Source LLC
Chambersburg PA
CBHW020714180526
45163CB00008B/3085